The Mealthy CrispLid Cookbook

Best One-Pot Pressure Cooker & Air Fryer Recipes For All Electric Pressure Cookers

PEACH MOORE

ISBN: 9781688911659

DEDICATION

For Ryan,

Pleasant memories, always!

TABLE OF CONTENTS

Also By Peach Moore

Easy Air Fryer Cookbook: Healthy and Tasty Air Fryer Recipes for Quick Air Frying

Plant-Based Diet Meal Plan: A 30-Day Plant-Based Meal-Plan For Better Health

The Hearty Spiralizer Cookbook: Over 100 Delectable Recipes For Paleo, Low Carb, Gluten-Free, Dairy Free, Weight Loss & Other Healthy Diets

INTRODUCTION

We all love pressure cooking. It is a fast, energy-saving, and healthier way to cook. It tenderizes food, adds extra flavor and makes it possible to cook several types of foods at the same time. Nevertheless, we still crave French fries, Mac and Cheese, crispy and browned chicken breasts, steaks, cheeseburgers and many similar healthy low-fat meals with that come with air frying.

The Mealthy CrispLid is here to here to bridge the gap between these two favorable cooking methods. It turns your Pressure Cooker into an Air Fryer, solving your crisping, broiling and air-frying needs. This amazing detachable lid works with any brand of 6 quart or 8 quart pressure cooker with a stainless steel inner pot. So if you have a Mealthy Pressure Cooker (of course!), an Instant Pot or Power Quick Pot cooker, you can make use of this revolutionary kitchen appliance.

The CrispLid sits on top of the stainless steel inner pot of your pressure cooker to perform 2 main function: 1. it crisp foods after pressure cooking; (think of pasta with melted cheese or pressure cooked ribs and carnitas that requires crisping afterwards). 2. It serves as a stand- alone air fryer. So, instead of getting an air fryer, you can simply use your CrispLid to air-fry your favorite foods.

The Mealthy CrispLid consists of the main housing with control panel, heating element and a fan that's attached to a glass lid. The heating element provides the air frying function of browning, crisping or air frying the foods inside it. The fan circulates the heat while the glass lid that it is attached to, helps to see and monitor your food while it's cooking. Other necessary tools, such as the handle, is used to place the CrispLid directly on top of any stainless steel pressure cooking pot of 6- or 8 quart. Not forgetting the control panel with its 6 buttons (temperature, time, +/-, stop, and start) and an LED screen to display the most recent time or temperature.

Upon purchase, the CrispLid comes with

- A 3 inch metal trivet (for air frying)
- An Air frying/broiling basket (for air frying))
- A silicone trivet/mat (for placing the Crisplid when it is hot; during cooking and after cooking)
- Stainless steel tongs (for removing fryer basket)
- User Manual and Recipe Booklet

...that simplifies the cooking process, making it so easy.

To use:

1. Unplug your pressure cooker.

2. Place the inner steel pot of your 6 or 8 quart pressure cooker into the base.

3. Place the trivet (either pressure cooker or Crisplid trivet) in the pot, and the fryer basket (if using) on it.

4. Lower the Crisplid on the steel pot until you hear it click into place. Select a cooking temperature by pressing the temperature button (it goes from 300 - 500°F in 25 degree increments). Next, select a cooking time (from 1 - 60 minutes) and then Press the start button (triangle) to begin.

5. Once the cooking cycle is complete and the food attains it desired crispiness, turn off the CrispLid and place it immediately on the silicon trivet to cool.

Most cooking times require that you flip the food or shake the basket during cooking. To do this, remove the CrispLid, place it on the silicon trivet and turn the food carefully with a tong and silicon mitts. As the Crisplid is removed, cooking will pause for several seconds and will immediately resume if the handle is placed backed. But if the lid is left off for too long and placed back, the cooking cycle will need to be reset. So it is best to always remember how much time is left on your meal before removing the lid.

Remember also that the handle must be turned down to activate the Crisplid and you must hit the triangle start button to start the cycle. If cooking above 450F, the maximum cooking time is 20 minutes and the inner steel pot and CrispLid must be left to cool for 10- 20 minutes before cooking. Temperatures below 450F have a maximum cook time of 60 minutes. Additionally, always place the hot CrispLid on the silicon trivet that comes with it, or any heat-resistant surface.

Pros of the Mealthy Crisplid

1. it's amazing! It works as intended and produces results just like any air fryer would.

2. It comes with a glass lid, enabling you see and monitor the progress of your food as it cooks.

3. It has a maximum temperature of 500F. Unlike most air fryers that has a maximum temperature of just 400F. This is a great added advantage.

4. It is safe to use. It comes with several safety precautions that guarantees the safety of the user. For example, it wouldn't work if the handle is not properly down in place. This makes it impossible for you to accidentally switch on the appliance and burn something in the process. Ensure also that you do not fill your inner pot above the max fill line. Nevertheless, ensure you read through the manual to get to know and understand more about the safety and user instructions.

Cons

1. The CrispLid can only be used with a 6 or 8 quart pressure cooker. Any other size could damage it.

2. It could also damage aluminum, ceramic, or nonstick coatings. It must always sit on top of a stainless steel inner pot.

3. The fryer basket holds a reasonable amount of foods. You may need to cook in batches to crisp food for a larger family.

4. You must toss or shake basket quickly and lock the handle back in place. Otherwise, the cook time will restart.

Overall, this cookbook will provide you with the pleasurable experience of pressuring cooking and air frying your food or just simply air frying them. There are best recipes that you will want to try over and over again with your Mealthy CrispLid. I hope you will find it exciting and rewarding.

BREAKFAST

Cajun Breakfast Sausage
A healthy breakfast that's perfect for all.

Prep Time: 15minutes

Cook Time: 40minutes

Servings: 13

Ingredients

11/2 lbs. ground sausage, chilled

1 teaspoon chili flakes

2 teaspoon fresh thyme leaves or ¾ of teaspoon dried thyme

1 teaspoon onion powder

1/2 teaspoon paprika

1/2 teaspoon cayenne

1/4 teaspoon sea salt & black pepper

Chopped sage (optional)

2 teaspoon maple syrup or brown sugar

3 teaspoon garlic, minced

2 teaspoon Tabasco

Herbs to garnish optional

Directions

1. Combine the ground sausage, together with the spices and herbs in a bowl, and mix well with hands. Add the tabasco sauce.

2. Form into patties of about 3 inches in width and 1 inch in thickness. Transfer to a lined baking tray so it doesn't stick. Place in the air fryer basket, in batches.

3. Place the pressure cooker trivet in the inner steel pot. Place the basket on the trivet. Place the Crisplid on top of the inner pot and plug it in. Set to 370°F for 20 minutes. Flip halfway and keep cooking.

4. Remove to a plate and cover. Cook the rest of the patties. Serve with sauce.

Per Serving: Calories 126; Total Fat 4.4g; Protein 11.2g; Total Carb 11g; Cholesterol: 45mg Fiber: 0.8g

Crustless Quiche

A versatile recipe that consist of adding together ingredients and quick cooking in your CrispLid. What a refreshing morning breakfast!

Prep Time: 10 minutes

Cook Time: 30 minutes

Serves: 4

Ingredients

1/2 cup Kalamata olives, chopped

4 large eggs

1/4 cup onion, chopped

1/2 cup of milk

1/2 cup tomatoes, chopped

1 cup of feta cheese, crumbled

1 tbsp. of basil, chopped

1 tbsp. oregano, chopped

2 tablespoon of canola oil

Salt & pepper

Directions

1. Coat a 6- inch pan with oil.

2. Whisk the eggs in a bowl and add the milk. Whisk to mix and add the salt and pepper for seasoning. Add the remaining ingredients, mix thoroughly and pour into greased pan.

3. Place the pressure cooker trivet in the inner pot of the cooker. Place the pan of egg mixture on it. Place the Crisplid on top of the inner pot and plug it in.

4. Set temperature to cook at 325°F for about 20 minutes until set. Enjoy!

Per Serving: Calories 406; Total Fat 29g; Protein 20g; Total Carb 14g; Cholesterol: 220mg/ Fiber: 1g

Tomato Frittata
Healthy and delicious!

Prep Time: 10 minutes

Cook Time: 15 minutes

Serves: 6

Ingredients

6 oz. canned tomatoes, finely chopped

6 large eggs, beaten

2 tablespoons of chopped parsley

2 tablespoons of chives, chopped

1/2 cup of shredded cheddar cheese

6 tablespoons of soft cream cheese

Cooking spray

Salt &pepper to taste

Directions

1. Add together all the ingredients, and mix to combine well.

2. Place the trivet in the inner pot and place a greased non-stick pan on it. Pour the mixture to spread evenly in the pan on the trivet.

3. Place the Crisp-lid on top of the inner pot and plug in. Set temperature to 350F and cook 15 minutes. Enjoy!

Per Serving: Calories 225; Total Fat 15g; Protein 11g; Net Carb 19g;

Breakfast Air Fried Potatoes

Crispy on the outside yet tender inside!

Prep Time: 5minutes

Cook Time: 20 minutes

Servings: 2

Ingredients

2 medium Russet Potatoes

1/2 teaspoon of salt

Cooking spray

1/4 teaspoon garlic powder

Chopped parsley for garnish

Directions

1. Begin by cleaning the potatoes and scrub them under running water. Cut into cubes of ½ inches.

2. Transfer to a bowl and add ice cold water to cover potatoes. Let it soak for 45minutes to 1 hr. Remove and pat dry with paper towels. Place in a dry bowl and add the rest of the ingredients, tossing well to mix.

3. Place in fryer basket. Place the trivet in the inner pot of your pressure cooker and place the basket on it. Place the Crisp-lid on top of the inner pot and plug in.

4. Set temperature to 400F and cook 20 minutes. Shake halfway and cook until the potatoes are golden brown and soft on the inside. Enjoy, topped with parsley!

Per Serving: Calories 146; Total Fat 0g; Protein 4g; Total Carb 32g; Cholesterol: 0mg Fiber: 3g

French Fries With Cheese & Gravy

Also called Poutine, this French savory dish is eaten with great gusto.

Prep Time: 15 minutes

Cook Time: 45minutes

Serves: 6

Ingredients

1 1/2 lb. Idaho potatoes, sliced thickly

6 cups of cold water

2 tablespoons olive oil

4 tablespoons butter

1/4 cup all-purpose flour

1 1/4 cups chicken stock

2 1/2 cups beef stock

1 tablespoon apple cider vinegar

2 tablespoon ketchup

2 teaspoons Worcestershire sauce

1 teaspoon salt

1/2 teaspoon ground black pepper

1 tablespoon cornstarch

2 cups fresh mozzarella cheese, diced

Directions

1. Soak fries in water for 30- 45 minutes. Drain and pat dry fries and toss with oil and then add to the crisping basket.

12

2. Place the pressure cooker trivet in the inner steel pot. Place the basket of fries on the trivet. Place the Crisplid on top of the inner pot and plug it in. Set to 390°F for 30 minutes. Half way through, open lid, place on the silicon trivet and toss. Replace lid.

3. Cook in batches, if necessary, and when done. Remove basket and trivet and set aside. Remove CrispLid, and unplug.

4. Plug in your pressure cooker. Preheat for 5 minutes on sauté and then melt the butter. Add the flour and stir until golden brown. Gently add in the beef and then the chicken stock and whisk to smoothness. Add ketchup, Worcestershire sauce, vinegar, salt and pepper.

5. Boil and cook on low temperature for 10 minutes. Combine cornstarch with a tablespoon of water, and add to the sauce, stirring until thickened. Serve fries, with cheese and gravy.

Per Serving: Calories 365; Total Fat 21g; Protein 14g; Total Carb 30g; Cholesterol: 51mg Fiber: 2g

Baked Egg Cups With Spinach & Cheese

Delicious, super quick and simple!

Prep Time: 5 minutes

Cook Time: 10minutes

Serves: 1

Ingredients

1 large egg

1 tablespoon milk or half & half

1 tablespoon frozen spinach, thawed

1-2 teaspoons grated cheese

Salt & black pepper, to taste

Cooking Spray

Directions

1. Spray muffin cups or ramekin with cook spray. Add the egg, milk, cheese, spinach and cheese in it. Add salt and pepper to season and stir gently without breaking the egg yolks.

2. Place in the fryer basket. Place the pressure cooker trivet in the inner steel pot. Place the basket of ramekins on the trivet. Place the Crisplid on top of the inner pot and plug it in. Set to 330°F for 10 minutes, checking every 5 minutes.

3. Cook egg to desired texture.

Per Serving: Calories 86; Total Fat 5g; Protein 7g; Total Carb 2g; Cholesterol: 188mg Fiber: 0g

Kale - Egg Frittata

A great main dish to relish!

Prep Time: 5 minutes

Cook Time: 15 minutes

Servings: 6

Ingredients

11/2 cup of kale, chopped

1/4 cup of parmesan cheese, grated

6 large eggs

1 cup of water

2 tablespoons of heavy cream

1/2 teaspoon of nutmeg, freshly grated

Salt and pepper, to taste

Directions

1. Combine the eggs, cream, nutmeg as well as the salt and pepper in a bowl, mixing until smooth. Add the kale and cheese and stir to mix well.

2. Lightly grease a round pan with cooking spray. Transfer the egg mix into it. Place the pressure cooker trivet in the inner steel pot. Place the pan on the trivet. Place the Crisplid on top of the inner pot and plug it in. Set to 350°F for 15 minutes.

Per Serving: Calories 137; Total Fat 8g; Protein 10g; Total Carb 7g; Cholesterol: 196mg Fiber: 2g

Toasted Cheese Sandwich

Enjoy this toasted sandwich with ham and tomato for a satisfying breakfast!

Prep Time: 5 minutes

Cook Time: 7 minutes

Servings: 1

Ingredients

2 bread slices

1 cheese slice

1 slice ham

2 tbsp butter

2 slices tomato

1 long toothpick

Directions

1. Assemble the sandwich, ensuring it is well buttered on the outside. Place a toothpick through, so the bread does not fly when being cooked.

2. Place in the fryer basket. Place the pressure cooker trivet in the inner steel pot. Place the basket on the trivet. Place the Crisplid on top of the inner pot and plug it in. Set to 390°F for 7- 10 minutes.

Per Serving: Calories 297; Total Fat 9.8g; Protein 20.9g; Total Carb 27.7g; Fiber: 4g

Air Fried Shirred Eggs

Prep Time: 5minutes

Cook Time: 17 minutes

Servings: 2

Ingredients

2 teaspoons unsalted butter

2 thin slices Black Forest ham

2 tablespoons heavy cream

4 large eggs

¾ teaspoon kosher salt

¼ teaspoon ground black pepper

3 tablespoons Parmesan cheese, finely grated

⅛teaspoon smoked paprika

2 teaspoons chopped fresh chives

Toasted bread, for serving (optional)

Directions

1. Butter a pie pan with butter and line with ham slices to cover the pan completely. Transfer pan to fryer basket.

2. In a bowl, break an egg and add the heavy cream, together with ¼ teaspoon of salt and a pinch of black pepper. Whisk to mix and then pour into the pie pan, directly over the ham. Break the remaining 3 eggs on top. Add salt and pepper to season and sprinkle over with Parmesan cheese.

3. Set trivet in the inner steel pot of your pressure cooker and place the basket of pie pan on top. Place the Crisplid on top of the inner pot and plug it in. Set to 320°F and 12 minutes cook time.

4. Remove shirred eggs with a spatula and transfer to plate, enjoyed season with Pimento and garnished with the shaved chives.

Per Serving: Calories 276; Total Fat 22g; Protein 18g; Total Carb 2g; Cholesterol: 414mg Fiber: 0g

Breakfast Casserole

Prep Time: 10 minutes

Cook Time: 20 minutes

Servings: 6

Ingredients

3 cups hash browns

1/2 lb. ground turkey breakfast sausage

6 eggs

1/2 cup milk

1/4 teaspoon black pepper

1/2 teaspoon kosher salt

1 cup shredded Colby cheese

Directions

1. In your pressure cooker inner steel pot, brown the sausage on sauté mode and then remove to a plate. Turn off pressure cooker.

2. Combine the eggs, milk, salt and pepper in a bowl. Grease a baking dish lightly, add the hash browns to it and sprinkle the sausage over it. Pour the egg mix over it, sprinkle over with cheese.

3. Place the pressure cooker trivet in the inner steel pot. Place the basket on the trivet. Place the Crisplid on top of the inner pot and plug it in. Set to 375°F for 15 minutes, checking frequently. Serve!

Per Serving: Calories 264; Total Fat 16g; Protein 20g; Total Carb 10g; Fiber: 1g; Cholesterol: 236mg

Beef Recipes

Crispy Sesame Beef

No need to eat out. This crispy beef recipe, made with little oil and cornstarch, is simply amazing!

Prep Time: 10minutes

Cook Time: 30 minutes

Serves: 4

Ingredients

Cooking spray

1 lb. sirloin steak, sliced thinly into strips

4 tbsp of cornstarch, divided

Sauce:

2 tablespoons of orange juice, freshly squeezed

1/4 cup reduced sodium soy sauce

1/4 cup brown sugar, packed

2 tablespoons rice vinegar

2 cloves garlic, minced

1 tablespoon ginger, freshly grated

1 tablespoon Sriracha

1 teaspoon sesame seeds

1 teaspoon sesame oil

1 green onion, thinly sliced

Directions:

1. Add together the steak and 2 tbsp cornstarch in a bowl, tossing well to coat. Add the remaining cornstarch to the bowl.

2. Place the steaks in the fryer basket in a single layer, spray with cooking spray and set the trivet in the pot of the pressure cooker. Place the fryer basket on the trivet and then set the Crisp lid on the pot and plug it in.

3. Set temperature to 500°F and cook for 5 minutes; flip and cook again for 5 minutes. (Work in batches). Remove lid and place on silicon trivet. Transfer steak to plate. Wipe the inner pot clean.

4. Set the pressure cooker on sauté mode over medium temperature. Add the sesame oil, soy sauce, orange juice, brown sugar, ginger, vinegar, garlic, and Sriracha in the pot. Let it cook and thicken for a minute or two.

5. Add the crispy steak and toss mixture gently to combine. Turn off saute and serve, garnished with sesame seeds and spring onions and enjoyed with boiled rice.

Nutrition info: Calories 367.8; Total Fat 17.6g; Protein 26.8g; Total Carb 24.6g; Dietary Fiber: 0.2g

Super Easy Steak

Super easy steak for your delight; cook appropriately though. If steaks are over 1-inch thick, cook 10 minutes or more. If 2 inches thick, cook 20 minutes and if an inch thick, just cook 5 minutes.

Prep Time: 5minutes

Cook Time: 10minutes

Serves: 2

Ingredients

2 (8 oz) ribeye steaks, boneless

1 tablespoon steak seasoning of choice

1 tablespoon unsalted butter

1 teaspoon kosher salt

Directions

1. Rub the steaks with the seasoning and salt. Let it rest for about 30 minutes to marinate well.

2. Place the steaks in the fryer basket in a single layer, and set the trivet in the pot of the pressure cooker. Place the fryer basket on the trivet and then set the Crisp lid on the pot and plug it in.

3. Set temperature to 500°F and cook for 5 minutes; flip and cook again for 5 minutes. Transfer to a cutting board and add 1½ teaspoons of butter to each of the steak. Let it rest 5-7 minutes and then slice.

4. Enjoy with greens of choice along with boiled rice.

Nutrition info: Calories 176; Total Fat 14g; Protein 11g; Net Carb 1.8g;

Air Fried Beef Satay

Prep Time: 35minutes

Cook Time: 8minutes

Serving: 2

Ingredients

1 lb. beef flank steak, sliced thinly

2 tablespoons canola oil

1 tablespoon soy sauce

1 tbsp fish sauce

1 tbsp minced ginger,

1 tablespoon garlic, minced

1 teaspoon Sriracha

1 tablespoon sugar

1 teaspoon ground coriander

1/2 cup of chopped cilantro, divided

1/4 cup of roasted peanuts, chopped

Directions

1. Get a Ziploc bag and add the beef strips to it, together with the fish sauce, canola oil, ginger, garlic, 1/4 cup of cilantro, coriander, Sriracha, soy sauce and sugar. Toss to combine well.

2. Marinate in the refrigerator for 30 minutes or up to 24 hours.

3. Coat the fryer basket with cook spray and then add the beef strip mixture to it, side by side. Set the Crisp lid trivet in the inner pot of your pressure cooker, place the fryer basket on top and set the Crisp lid on top of the inner pot. Plug in.

4. Cook for 8 minutes at 400°F, flip once halfway. Remove to a serving plate and top with the chopped roasted peanuts and chopped cilantro.

Nutrition info: Calories 803; Total Fat 46g; Protein 53g; Total Carb 40g; Dietary Fiber: 5g; Cholesterol:90mg

Beef Cheeseburger

Juicy and perfect for dinner!

Prep Time: 15 minutes

Cook Time: 15 minutes

Serves: 4

Ingredients

1 pound 80% of lean ground chuck

Freshly ground black pepper, to taste

Kosher salt, to taste

4 slices American cheese

4 burger buns

Condiments, optional: mayonnaise, ketchup and mustard

For toppings, optional:

Lettuce, red onion, tomato, and pickles

Directions

1. Combine ground chuck and a sprinkle of pepper and salt in a bowl and mix gently.

2. Divide into 4 equal parts and place the first portion in a plate. Press down to make a round patty of an inch. Do not make it smooth and too flat. Make an indentation of ¼-½ inch from the edge of the burger. Do this for all four burgers.

3. Coat the fryer basket with cook spray and then add the patties, in batches. Set the Crisp lid trivet in the inner pot of your pressure cooker, place the fryer basket on top and set the Crisp lid on top of the inner pot. Plug in.

27

4. Cook for 16 minutes at 375°F, flipping halfway with tongs. Use a meat thermometer to check that the center of the burger reads at least 165°F; and then remove.

5. 5 minutes to end of cook time, place the cheese on top of the burgers. Serve on toasted buns and top it with your favorite toppings. Enjoy!

Nutrition info: Calories 485; Total Fat 30g; Protein 27g; Total Carb 22g; Cholesterol: 101mg

Poultry Recipes

Tender & Crispy Lemon Rotisserie Chicken

A perfect family dinner of tender chicken with a crispy finishing. Enjoy the amazing wonders of your multi-cooker!

Prep Time: 5 minutes

Cook Time: 34 minutes

Servings: 4-6

Ingredients

1 (21/2 lb.) whole chicken

1 lemon, cut into 4 wedges

2 tablespoons of olive oil

1 teaspoon garlic powder

1 1/2 teaspoons salt

1 teaspoon paprika

1/2 teaspoon of ground black pepper

1 cup of chicken broth

Directions

1. Rinse the chicken, and pat dry with paper towel. Insert the lemon wedges inside the chicken cavity.

2. Combine the broth, paprika, salt, pepper and garlic in the pot. Place the chicken in the basket and place basket in the pot.

3. Place the pressure lid on and ensure the release valve is set to the sealing position. Cook on high pressure for 15 minutes. Quick release the pressure, open the lid and turn off pressure cooker.

4. Remove basket, drain inner pot, wipe dry and return. Place the pressure cooker trivet in the pot. Brush the chicken with the canola oil and place on trivet. Set the Crisplid on the pot and plug it in. Set temperature to cook at 400°F for 15 minutes. Flip halfway.

5. Remove chicken once desired doneness is attained. Let it rest for a few minutes before serving.

Nutrition info: Calories 284; Total Fat 18.8g; Protein 27.7g; Total Carb 2.9g

Crispy Baked Chicken Thighs

A one pot chicken dish that's crispy on the outside and remarkably tender and juicy on the inside.

Prep Time: 10 minutes

Cook Time: 35 minutes

Servings: 8

Ingredients

3 lb. chicken thighs

Cooking spray

2 teaspoons kosher salt

2 teaspoons garlic powder

2 teaspoons Italian seasoning

2 teaspoon onion powder

1 teaspoon paprika

1 teaspoon black pepper

Directions

1. Combine the salt, garlic powder, pepper, onion powder, paprika and Italian seasoning in a small bowl.

2. Pat dry chicken thighs, spray with cook spray lightly and sprinkle generously and evenly with the spices.

3. Place the thighs in the fryer basket, in batches. Ensure they are in a single layer. Set the Crisplid on the pot and plug it in. Set temperature to cook at 400°F for 40 minutes. Flip halfway.

4. Chicken is done when it attains and internal temperature of 165°F.

Nutrition info: Calories 401; Total Fat 31g; Protein 27g; Total Carb 2g; Cholesterol: 166mg

Crunchy BBQ Chicken Drumsticks

Easy and enjoyable crunchy barbecued chicken drumsticks that the whole family loves. Taste just like grilled chicken!

Prep Time: 45 minutes

Cook Time: 40 minutes

Servings: 12

Ingredients

4 lb chicken drumsticks (10- 12 pieces)

2 tablespoons onion powder

2 tablespoons garlic powder

2 tablespoons smoked paprika

2 tablespoons chili powder

1 tablespoon ground ginger

2 teaspoons kosher salt

1 teaspoon pepper

2 cups bbq sauce

Directions

1. Combine all the spices, except the chicken and bbq sauce, in a bowl and coat the chicken pieces in the dry rub.

2. Let it sit for about 30 minutes and then place in the fryer basket, in batches.

3. Set Crisp Lid trivet in pressure cooker inner steel pot and set fryer basket on it. Set Crisp Lid on pot and plug it in. Set to 375°F and cook 30 minutes, flipping every 10 minutes.

4. Remove chicken to a plate and slather with barbeque sauce. Wipe fat from the fryer basket and then place the bbq-coated chicken back in it.

5. Cook and flip for 5-10 minutes until crispy. Serve, with barbeque sauce for dipping.

Nutrition info: Calories 337; Total Fat 14g; Protein 38g; Total Carb 23g; Cholesterol: 192mg; Fiber: 2g

Whole Roast Chicken

This keto-friendly, paleo-friendly, healthy main dish recipe is so easy to make and ready within an hour!

Prep Time: 10 minutes

Cook Time: 1 hr 10minutes

Servings: 4

Ingredients

1 whole chicken (3 lb.)

1 tablespoon canola oil

1/4 teaspoon ground black pepper

1 teaspoon kosher salt

1 lemon, cut into 4

4 cloves garlic

Directions

1. Place the pressure cooker trivet in the inner pot, in the higher position (with trivet handles up).

2. Rinse chicken, remove giblets and pat dry. Rub with oil all over and season with salt and pepper. Stuff the cloves and lemon in the cavity of the chicken.

3. Place on the trivet in the inner pot with the breast side down and the legs and wings tucked under the chicken.

4. Set the Crisplid on the pot and plug it in. Set temperature to cook at 400°F for 40 minutes.

5. Remove Crisp lid and chicken as well by lifting the handles of the trivet. Flip with tongs and then lower chicken and trivet carefully back to pot, with the trivet handles.

6. Cook until a meat thermometer inserted reads at least 165°F. This should take another 30 to 40 minutes at the same temperature.

7. Cool 5 minutes, carve and enjoy!

Nutrition info: Calories 87; Total Fat 6g; Protein 6g; Net Carb 3g; Cholesterol: 20mg

Crispy Sausage Dinner
A weeknight favorite!

Prep Time: 5 minutes

Cook Time: 12 minutes

Servings: 4

Ingredients

4 Chicken Sausages

Cooking Spray

Directions

1. Spray basket. Place sausages in.

2. Place the trivet in the inner pot of pressure cooker. Place basket on trivet. Set the Crisplid on the pot and plug it in. Set temperature to cook at 350°F for 12 minutes, tossing halfway through.

Nutrition info: Calories 37; Total Fat 2g; Protein 4g; Net Carb 0g; Cholesterol: 17mg; Fiber: 0g

Cheesy Chicken

A satisfying touch to your day!

Prep Time: 10 minutes

Cook Time: 15 minutes

Servings: 6

Ingredients

Cooking spray

3/4 cup bread crumbs, Italian-styled

3 tablespoons Parmesan cheese, grated

3 tablespoons butter, melted

Salt &ground black pepper to taste

6 boneless, skinless chicken thighs

3/4 cup marinara sauce

3/4 cup mozzarella cheese

Directions

1. Spray basket with cooking spray.

2. Combine the bread crumbs and Parmesan cheese in a bowl. In a separate bowl, pour melted butter.

3. Brush the chicken thighs with the butter, season with salt and the black pepper and then dredge each of the thigh in the breadcrumb mixture to coat well.

4. Place in the basket and spray lightly with cooking spray. Set the trivet in the pressure cooker inner steel pot and place the fryer basket on top it. Now set the CrispLid on the inner pot and plug it in.

5. Set at 350°F for 7 minutes, flip and top each of the chicken with 2 tablespoons of marinara sauce and 2 tablespoons of shredded mozzarella cheese.

6. Keep cooking for another 7 minutes until it is no longer pink in the center. Enjoy with pasta.

Per Serving: Calories 335; Total Fat 17g; Protein 33g; Total Carb 13.3g; Cholesterol: 748mg;

Salsa Chicken

Frozen chicken breasts plus taco seasoning plus salsa prepared with your CrispLid, produce a flavorsome Mexican-themed meal.

Prep Time: 15 minutes

Cook Time: 30 minutes

Serves: 6

Ingredients

1 lb. frozen skinless, boneless chicken breast halves

1 (1 oz.) packet taco seasoning mix

1/2 cup salsa

1/2 cup low-sodium chicken broth

Directions

1. Place the chicken breast in pressure cooker basket. Place the basket in the pot.

2. Sprinkle the chicken with taco seasoning and pour the chicken broth and salsa over the chicken.

3. Place the pressure lid on and ensure that it is set to sealing. Cook on high pressure for 15 minutes. When time elapses, do a quick release and open carefully. Remove basket. Remove chicken and wipe dry. Turn off pressure cooker.

4. Spray chicken with cooking spray and place in air fryer basket. Set Crisp Lid trivet in pressure cooker inner steel pot and set fryer basket on it. Set Crisp Lid on pot and plug it in.

5. Set to 400°F and cook 15 minutes, flipping halfway

Per Serving: Calories 89; Total Fat 2g; Protein 15g; Total Carb 2g; Cholesterol: 37mg;

Crispy Chicken Burger

An easy to prepare homemade seasoned burger in less than an hour!

Prep Time: 10 minutes

Cook Time: 16 minutes

Serves: 6

Ingredients

1 1/2 lb ground chicken

3/4 cup of seasoned bread crumbs

6 tablespoons Parmesan cheese, grated

1 1/2 eggs, whisked

1 1/2 tablespoons fresh garlic, minced

1 1/2 teaspoons Worcestershire sauce

Cooking spray

Directions

1. In a bowl, add together the ground chicken, egg, Parmesan cheese, garlic and Worcestershire sauce and mix well to combine. Form into patties and chill for at least 25 minutes.

2. Coat the fryer basket with cook spray and then add the chicken patties, in batches. Set the Crisp lid trivet in the inner pot of your pressure cooker, place the fryer basket on top and set the Crisp lid on top of the inner pot. Plug in.

3. Cook for 16 minutes at 375°F, flipping halfway with tongs. Use a meat thermometer to check that the center of the burger reads at least 165°F; and then remove.

4. Enjoy, topped with favorite fixings and a beverage drink

Per Serving: Calories 320; Total Fat 16g; Protein 32g; Total Carb 12g; Cholesterol: 430mg

Buffalo Chicken Meatballs

Prep Time: 10 minutes

Cook Time: 20 minutes

Serves: 6

Ingredients

11/2 lb. ground chicken

3/4 cup almond meal

1 teaspoon of sea salt

2 garlic cloves, minced

2 green onions, thinly sliced

2 tablespoons of ghee

6 tablespoons of hot sauce

4 tablespoons of butter, melted in the microwave

Chopped green onions, for garnish

Directions

1. Add together the chicken, almond meal, garlic cloves, green onions and salt in a large bowl and combine thoroughly with your hands.

2. Grease hands with coconut oil and shape into 1-2 inches wide meatballs. Place the meatballs in the inner pot of your pressure cooker and sauté in 2 tablespoons of butter until brown on all sides. Remove and set aside. Turn off pressure cooker.

3. Place the pressure cooker trivet in the pot and place the fryer basket on it. Add the meatballs to the basket, and add the melted butter and hot sauce on top. Set the Crisp Lid on the pot and plug it in.

4. Cook at 400°F for15 minutes. Enjoy with cauliflower rice or zoodles.

Per Serving: Calories 247; Total Fat 22g; Protein 8g; Total Carb 3g; Cholesterol: 20mg; Fiber:2g

Crispy Cajun Chicken Breasts

Just a jar of salt-free Cajun seasoning and a few pats of butter and you have yourself a dinner of a rich, juicy, beautiful golden-brown chicken you want to keep eating!

Prep Time: 5 minutes

Cook Time: 35 minutes

Serves: 4

Ingredients

3 tablespoons unsalted butter

1 tablespoon Cajun seasoning blend, salt-free

1 teaspoon of kosher salt

4 boneless, skinless chicken breasts (about 2 lb all)

Directions

1. In a small bowl, add together the melted butter, Cajun seasoning, and salt and mix thoroughly to combine.

2. Pat dry the chicken and place in the trivet basket, (cook in batches). Brush the chicken on all sides with the butter & spice mixture.

3. Set the trivet in the pressure cooker pot and place the fryer basket on top it. Now set the CrispLid on the inner pot and plug it in.

4. Cook 25-35 minutes at 425°F. Half way through cooking, flip and brown the other side.

Per Serving: Calories 406; Total Fat 15.8g; Protein 61.4g; Total Carb 0.7g;

BBQ Chicken Sausage Pizza
A fusion of Indian and Italian cuisine!

Prep Time: 10 minutes

Cook Time: 8minutes

Serves: 1

Ingredients

1 piece naan bread

Cooking spray

1/4 cup barbeque sauce

1/8 cup pineapple tidbits, drained

1/4 cup shredded mozzarella cheese

1/4 cup shredded cheddar cheese

1/8 small red onion, sliced thinly

1/2 chicken sausage, thinly sliced

Chopped fresh cilantro, for garnish

Directions

1. Spray the bottom of the bread with cooking spray and place on the fryer basket.

2. Spread with BBQ sauce and then top with the mozzarella cheese and the cheddar cheese and spread the rest of the toppings on top. Spray lightly with cooking spray

3. Set the trivet in the pressure cooker pot and place the fryer basket on top it. Now set the CrispLid on the inner pot and plug it in.

4. Set to cook at 400°F for 7-8 minutes. Cool and serve, topped with cilantro.

Per Serving: Calories 626; Total Fat 21g; Protein 30g; Total Carb 77.7g; Cholesterol: 1765mg

Pork Recipes

Pork Chops & Broccoli
Juicy and ready in a bit!

Prep Time: 15 minutes

Cook Time: 15 minutes

Servings: 2

Ingredients

2- 1/2 oz. bone-in pork chops

2 tablespoons avocado oil

1/2 teaspoon onion powder

1/2 teaspoon paprika

1/2 teaspoon garlic powder

1 teaspoon salt, divided

2 cloves garlic, minced

2 cups broccoli florets

Directions

1. Drizzle both sides of the pork chops with a tablespoon of oil. Season with onion powder, paprika, garlic powder and 1/2 teaspoon of salt.

2. Spray fryer basket with cook spray and then place seasoned pork chops in it. Set the trivet in the pressure cooker pot and place the fryer basket on top it. Now set the CrispLid on the inner pot and plug it in. Set to cook at 350°F for 10 minutes.

3. Meanwhile, combine in a bowl; the broccoli, the garlic, the /2 teaspoon salt that's left and remaining tablespoon of oil and toss to coat.

4. Once cooking time elapses, add the broccoli to the basket and keep cooking for 5 minutes, flipping halfway. Serve!

Per Serving: Calories 483; Total Fat 30g; Protein 40g; Total Carb 12g; Cholesterol: 119mg; Fiber:6g

Crispy Breaded Pork Chops

Moist on the inside yet crispy on the outside!

Prep Time: 5 minutes

Cook Time: 12 minutes

Servings: 6

Ingredients

Cooking spray

6 3/4-inch thick (5 oz. each) center cut boneless pork chops, trimmed of fat

Kosher salt

1 large egg, beaten

1/2 cup panko crumbs

1/3 cup crushed cornflakes crumbs

2 tbsp. parmesan cheese, grated

1 1/4 teaspoon of sweet paprika

1/2 teaspoon of garlic powder

1/2 teaspoon of onion powder

1/4 teaspoon of chili powder

1/8 teaspoon of black pepper

Directions

1. Spray fryer basket with cooking spray lightly.

2. Season pork chops with ½ teaspoon of salt on both sides. Add together the cornflake crumbs, panko, onion powder, garlic powder, chili powder,

paprika, 3/4 tsp kosher salt, and black pepper as well as parmesan cheese in a large bowl.

3. Whisk egg in a separate bowl.

4. Dip the pork in the egg and then in the crumb mixture. Place 3 of the pork chops in the fryer basket and spritz top with spray.

5. Set the trivet in the pressure cooker pot and place the fryer basket on top it. Now set the CrispLid on the inner pot and plug it in. Set to cook at 425°F for 12 minutes, flipping halfway.

6. Repeat process with the remaining chops.

Per Serving: Calories 378; Total Fat 13g; Protein 33g; Total Carb 8g; Cholesterol: 121mg;

Fish And Seafood

Cajun Butter Baked Salmon

Cajun butter is simply delicious and when added to salmon and baked in your Crisplid, makes a perfect dinner for family and friends.

Prep Time: 15 minutes

Cook Time: 30 minutes

Servings: 8

Ingredients

2 lemons, sliced into rounds

1 large salmon fillet

Kosher salt & freshly ground black pepper

4 tbsp butter, melted

3 cloves garlic, minced

2 tablespoons of whole-grain mustard

2 teaspoons of Cajun seasoning

1 tsp. fresh thyme leaves

Pinch of crushed red pepper flakes

Thinly sliced green onions, for serving

Directions

1. Place the lemon rounds in a steel pan, in an even layer. Place the salmon on top and add salt and pepper to season.

2. In a small bowl, add together the melted butter, mustard, garlic, Cajun seasoning, red pepper flakes and thyme and then brush all over the salmon.

3. Place pressure cooker trivet in inner pot and place the pan on the trivet. Set the Crisp lid on the pot and plug it.

5. Set to cook at 350°F for 30 minutes and then toss halfway. Cook until butter mixture has thickened. Serve, garnished with green onions.

Per Serving: Calories 98; Total Fat 8g; Protein 4g; Total Carb 3g; Cholesterol: 25mg; Fiber: 0g

Classic Fish And Chips

No deep frying; just toss potatoes in little oil, coat fish in batter and there you go! Enjoy with favorite dipping sauce as dinner.

Prep Time: 15 minutes

Cook Time: 30minutes

Serving: 2

Ingredients

2 large potatoes, peeled & cut into strips

½ cup all-purpose flour

1 teaspoon baking powder

½ teaspoon salt

½ teaspoon ground black pepper

Cooking Spray

½ cup milk

1 egg

1 tablespoon olive oil

3/4 lb. cod fillets

Directions

1. In a bowl, combine the flour, baking powder, salt, and pepper. Add the milk and egg; stir until smooth. Let it stand for 20 minutes.

2. Combine potatoes and oil in a bowl and toss for even coating. Season with salt and black pepper.

3. Spray fryer basket with cooking spray. Place potatoes in a single layer in the basket. Set the Crisp lid trivet in the inner pot of your pressure cooker,

place the fryer basket on top and set the Crisp lid on top of the inner pot. Plug in.

4. Set to 400°F and cook for 20 minutes, flipping halfway through cooking. Remove, cover and set aside.

5. Dredge the fillet, one at a time in the whisked batter. Arrange evenly in the fryer basket and cook for 10 minutes. Flip halfway and cook until the outside is crispy yet the inside is fully cooked.

6. Return potato fries to basket and cook for a couple of minutes to heat through. Serve!

Per Serving: Calories 490; Total Fat 16g; Protein 32g; Total Carb 56g; Cholesterol: 191mg; Fiber: 4g

Honey Salmon and Asparagus With Cauli Rice

Healthy and good for you, this tasty lunch or dinner dish of well-marinated crispy salmon with sautéed cauliflower rice and greens is ready in a matter of minutes.

Prep Time: 5 minutes

Cook Time: 20 minutes

Serves: 4

Ingredients

3 tablespoons low-sodium soy sauce

6 tablespoons mirin

2 tablespoons honey

1 pound fresh wild salmon fillet, cut in 4

Cooking spray

12 oz. asparagus, ends trimmed & then cut

4 cups riced cauliflower

1 tablespoon olive oil

Sesame seeds, for garnish

Directions

1. Add together the mirin, soy sauce and the honey in a Ziploc bag. Add the salmon and mix to ensure thorough coating. Chill in the refrigerator for 1 to 8 hours.

2. Remove the salmon, but reserve the marinade. Spray salmon generously with cooking spray and place skin-side-down (in batches) in the fryer basket, Toss the asparagus with a little oil and season with salt. Add the asparagus (in batches) to the salmon in the fryer basket.

3. Set the trivet in the pressure cooker pot and place the fryer basket on top it. Now set the CrispLid on the inner pot and plug it in.

4. Set to 400°F and cook 10 minutes or until fish flakes easily with a fork.

5. Meanwhile, simmer the marinade in a small pot for about 7 minutes until thickened.

6. Add oil to a large skillet and, and once warm, add cauliflower rice and cook, with constant stirring, for about 5 minutes until tender.

7. To serve, divide the cauliflower rice in bowls, top it with salmon and the asparagus and drizzle with the glaze. Sprinkle with sesame seeds.

Per Serving: Calories 324; Total Fat 13g; Protein 24.5g; Total Carb 27g; Cholesterol: 46.5mg; Fiber: 4g

Parmesan Crusted Lemon Pepper Tilapia

This would be one of the best tilapia recipe you've ever tasted! So delicious, healthy and super easy!

Prep Time: 5 minutes

Cook Time: 15 minutes

Serves: 4

Ingredients

4 tilapia filets, about 4 oz each

1 /4 cup Parmesan cheese, grated

1/8 teaspoon salt

1 tablespoon lemon pepper

1 tablespoon parsley, chopped

Cooking spray

1/4 cup of shredded Parmesan

For optional garnish:

Lemon wedges

1/4 cup of diced green onions

Directions

1. Add together the grated parmesan cheese, lemon pepper, salt and parsley in a bowl. Coat the tilapia with the cheese mixture and spray with cooking spray. Press lightly to ensure it sticks and finally sprinkle the tilapia with the shredded parmesan. Place in the trivet basket.

2. Set the trivet in the pressure cooker pot and place the fryer basket on top it. Now set the CrispLid on the inner pot and plug it in.

3. Set to 400°F and bake10 minutes or until the fish is opaque in the thickest part and cheese crust is a little crispy.

4. Top with green onions and serve, if desired with lemon wedges.

Per Serving: Calories 263; Total Fat 11g; Protein 40g; Total Carb 2g; Cholesterol: 85mg; Fiber: 0g

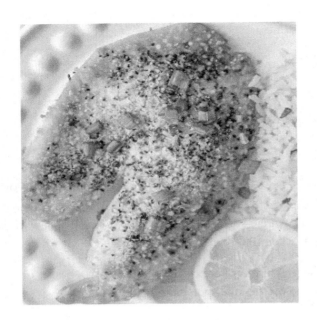

Lemon Pepper Salmon With Cauliflower Rice

A quick baked salmon recipe.

Prep Time: 10minutes

Cook Time: 20 minutes

Serves: 2

Ingredients

2 4 oz. wild salmon fillet

1 lemon

Pink salt & black pepper

Cauliflower

2 teaspoons olive oil

1 head cauliflower, chopped in about 1/2-inch pieces

1-2 cloves garlic chopped small

Pink salt & black pepper

2 tablespoons of water

Directions

1. Place the fillets in the fryer basket. Zest the lemon into a bowl and set to one side. Cut the lemons into 4 and then squeeze 2 quarters over a salmon.

2. Coat the fillets generously with pink salt and pepper and add some lemon zest, reserving the rest.

3. Set the trivet in the pressure cooker pot and place the fryer basket on top it. Now set the CrispLid on the inner pot and plug it in. Set to 400°F for 12-15 minutes, depending on thickness.

4. Meanwhile, pulse the chopped cauliflower in a food processor or blender, until it's rice-like.

5. To save time, add oil to a heated pan and sauté the garlic until fragrant. Add the cauliflower rice and then the black pepper, salt and water. Stir and cook until the cauliflower rice is soft, about 7 minutes.

6. Finally, ladle the cauliflower rice on to a plate, top with lemon zest or juice and ten place the crispy salmon on top. Enjoy, if desired with extra lemon wedges.

Per Serving: Calories 276; Total Fat 7g; Protein 24g; Total Carb 39g; Cholesterol: 23mg; Fiber: 17g

Shrimp & Chessy Butter Grits

Prep Time: 10 minutes

Cook Time: 14 minutes

Servings: 4

Ingredients

3 cups water, divided

1 cup grits

3 teaspoons kosher salt, divided

16 uncooked jumbo shrimp, frozen

Juice of 1 lemon

1 teaspoon extra virgin olive oil

2 garlic cloves, peeled & minced

1 teaspoon chili powder

1 teaspoon black pepper

1 teaspoon garlic powder

1/4 cup butter, cut in pieces of 8

1/4 cup of grated Parmesan cheese, grated

2 tablespoons fresh parsley, chopped

2 scallions, thinly sliced

Directions

1. Peel shrimps, devein and pat dry. Pour ½ cup of water in the pressure cooker inner steel pot. In an 8 inch baking pan, add the rest of the water, the grits and 2 teaspoons of salt. Stir.

2. Now place the pan in a trivet or rack and place in pot. Seal pressure lid. Pressure cook 4 minutes on high and perform a 10 minutes natural release. Unplug pressure cooker.

3. Meanwhile, place the shrimp in a bowl and toss with olive oil, lemon juice, garlic, garlic powder, chili powder, pepper and the rest of the salt. Coat well and set aside.

4. Add cheese and butter to the grits in the pan. Lay the shrimps on the grits. Now set the CrispLid on the inner pot and plug it in. Set to 375°F for 10 minutes

5. Serve, garnished with scallions and parsley.

Per Serving: Calories 193; Total Fat 15g; Protein 5g; Total Carb 11g; Cholesterol: 43mg; Fiber: 1g

Simple Tuna Melt

A fancy open-faced sandwich that your friends and family will love. This simple easy meal has been made even simpler with your Crisplid. Enjoy for lunch or dinner.

Prep Time: 5minutes

Cook Time: 3minutes

Servings: 1

Ingredients

1 (5 ounce) can tuna, drained & flaked

2 tablespoons mayonnaise + more

1 teaspoon balsamic vinegar

1 pinch salt

1 teaspoon Dijon mustard

2 slices whole wheat bread

2 teaspoons dill pickle, chopped

2 thin slices of tomatoes

1/4 cup sharp Cheddar cheese, shredded

Directions

1. Combine in a small bowl; the tuna, mayo, salt, Dijon mustard, balsamic vinegar and dill pickle. Ensure it is evenly blended, and then pile the mixture on top of the slices of bread.

2. Top the open-face sandwiches with the tomatoes and cheese.

3. Place in the fryer basket, with the tuna-side up. Set the trivet in the pressure cooker and place the fryer basket on top of the trivet.

4. Place the Crisplid on top of the inner pot and plug it in. Cook on 500°F for 3 minutes until cheese is melted and the tuna is heated through.

Nutrition info: Calories 608; Total Fat 34.2g; Protein 46.8g; Total Carb26.8 8g; Cholesterol: 78 mg

Crispy Lemon Salmon

Restaurant-style prepared crispy salmon with just 3 ingredients is ready is about 15 minutes. Enjoy with a whole grain and vegetable.

Prep Time: 5 minutes

Cook Time: 5 minutes

Serves: 2

Ingredients

2 salmon fillets skin-on, rinsed and dried

Cooking spray

Salt & ground black pepper

2 teaspoon lemon juice

Directions

1. Coat the rinsed and dried salmon fillets with cooking spray generously on both sides; season with the salt and ground pepper and rub lemon juice all over fillets, rubbing in.

2. Place in the Crisp Lid basket with the skin side facing down.

3. Set the trivet in the pressure cooker pot and place the fryer basket on top it. Now set the CrispLid on the inner pot and plug it in.

4. Cook 10 minutes at 375°F. Serve and enjoy!

Per Serving: Calories 425; Total Fat 29g; Protein 40g; Cholesterol: 109mg

Cajun Shrimp Dinner

A hearty meal of shrimp, sausages and colorful veggies.

Prep Time: 10 minutes

Cook Time: 20 minutes

Servings: 4

Ingredients

1 tablespoon seasoning, Creole or Cajun

24 (1 lb.) extra jumbo shrimp, cleaned & peeled

6 oz. cooked Andouille sausage, sliced

1 medium zucchini, 8 ounces, sliced thickly into 1/4-inch half moons

1 medium yellow squash, 8 ounces, sliced thickly into 1/4-inch half moons

1 large red bell pepper, seeded & cut thinly into 1-inch pieces

1/4 teaspoon of kosher salt

2 tablespoons of olive oil

Directions

1. Add together the seasoning and shrimp in a bowl. Toss to coat and then add the sausage, squash, zucchini, the bell peppers, and salt. Add the oil and toss.

2. Place in batches in the fryer basket. Place trivet in the inner steel pot and place the basket on it. Set at 400F and 10 minutes cook time, tossing halfway through cooking.

3. Repeat with the reserved shrimp and veggies.

Per Serving: Calories 284; Carbs: 8g; Total Fat 14g; Protein 31g; Cholesterol: 205mg; Fiber: 2g

Other Recipes

Sweet, Salty And Meaty Bean Bake
A bean dish that is beyond the ordinary!

Prep Time: 15 minutes

Cook Time: 1 hr. 30 minutes

Servings: 8

Ingredients

1 lb. ground beef

1 lb bacon, cut into pieces

1 onion, chopped

1/2 cup brown sugar

1/4 cup of ketchup

2 tablespoons molasses

1/4 cup of bbq sauce

2 tablespoons mustard

1 15 oz can pork and beans

1 15 oz can kidney beans

1 15 oz can butter beans

Directions

1. Press the sauté function of your pressure cooker and brown the bacon pieces. Remove and set aside.

2. Add the diced onions and brown until translucent. Remove and set aside with the bacon.

3. Add the ground beef and brown and then set aside with the bacon and onions. Turn off pressure cooker.

4. Transfer the sautéed ingredients to a stainless steel casserole pan. Add the rest of the ingredients as well.

5. Place the trivet in the inner pot of the pressure cooker and place the casserole pan on it. Set the Crisp Lid on pot and plug it in. Set temperature to 350F and cook for an hour. Enjoy!

Per Serving: Calories 576; Carbs: 49g; Total Fat 26g; Protein 38g; Cholesterol: 87mg; Fiber: 7g

Cheese- Rich Green Bean Casserole

A quick and easy pressure-cooked green beans and mushroom recipe, topped with breadcrumbs and cheesy goodness.

Prep Time: 15 minutes

Cook Time: 20 minutes

Servings: 8

Ingredients

4 cups fresh green beans, without stems

1 can cream of mushroom soup

2 garlic cloves, chopped

1/2 cup mozzarella cheese, part skim, shredded

1 cup mozzarella cheese, part skim, cubed

1 cup sharp cheddar cheese, shredded

1/3 cup panko breadcrumbs

1 1/2 cup French fried onions

Salt and pepper

Cooking spray

1 tablespoon of flour

1 teaspoon water

1 teaspoon olive oil

Directions

1. Sauté the olive oil and garlic in the inner pot of pressure cooker until fragrant. Add the green beans and cream of mushroom soup and then season with salt and pepper.

2. Secure pressure cooker and cook on high pressure for 15 minutes. Perform a quick release, open lid and press the sauté function.

3. Create a slurry by mixing flour and water in a bowl. Add to the pot and add half of the shredded cheese, stir and let it cook for 2 minutes to melt cheese. Turn off pressure cooker.

4. Place the mozzarella cubes all over the casserole. Top with the rest of the shredded cheese, panko breadcrumbs, and the fried onions.

5. Set the Crisp lid on top of the inner pot. Plug in. Set to 450°F and cook the casserole 10 minutes until the bread crumbs are browned. Cool and serve.

Per Serving: Calories 275; Total Fat 18g; Protein 10g; Carbs: 15g

Black Bean Dip

Prep Time; 15 minutes

Cook Time: 10 minutes

Servings: 4 cups

Ingredients

2 cans black beans (151/2 oz. each), rinsed & drained

1 can (14.5 ounces) tomatoes, diced or crushed

1 onion, peeled & chopped

2 jalapeño peppers, chopped, deseeded

4 cloves garlic, peeled & chopped

2 tablespoons canola oil

1 1/2 teaspoons kosher salt

1 teaspoon chili powder

1 teaspoon ground cumin

1/2 teaspoon smoked paprika

2 tablespoons + more fresh lime juice

1/2 cup fresh cilantro leaves, chopped

1 cup of Monterey Jack cheese, shredded

Directions

1. Combine in the inner steel pot of your pressure cooker, the following: beans, tomatoes, jalapeño peppers, onion, garlic, salt, oil, cumin, smoked paprika and chili powder

2. Place lid in place and secure appropriately. Cook 5 minutes on high pressure and perform a quick release afterwards. Turn off the pressure cooker.

3. Blend with an immersion blender or mash to desired consistency. Add the cilantro and lime juice and stir to mix.

4. Sprinkle the shredded cheese over it. Place the Crisp lid on and plug it in. Broil for 5 minutes. Enjoy!

Per Serving: Calories 222; Carbs: 13g; Total Fat 16g; Protein 8g; Cholesterol: 25mg; Fiber: 3g

Asian Fried Cauliflower

Also known as Gobi Manchurian, this Asian dish is a family's favorite.

Prep Time: 15 minutes

Cook Time: 35 minutes

Servings: 6

Ingredients

1/2 cup of flour

1/2 teaspoon of baking powder

3 tablespoons of cornstarch

1 teaspoon chili powder

1/4 teaspoon sea salt

3/4 cup of water

1 head cauliflower, (4 cups), cut in florets

1 teaspoon sesame oil

1 teaspoon fresh ginger, minced

1 teaspoon garlic, minced

1 teaspoon chili paste

2 tablespoons soy sauce

3 tablespoons of chili sauce

2 tablespoons of ketchup

2 tablespoons fresh green onions, chopped

Directions

1. Add together the cornstarch, flour, baking powder, the chili powder and the salt in a large bowl. Add the water and whisk to form a thick batter.

2. Now add the cauliflower and stir to ensure even coating. Remove coated cauliflower to a sheet tray. Freeze for an hour.

3. Press the sauté function of your pressure cooker and then add oil. Sauté garlic and ginger for a minute. Add the rest of the ingredients but not the green onions. Cook to thicken for a couple of minutes. Remove to a bowl. Wipe out inner pot with a paper towel.

4. When an hour has elapsed, remove cauliflower from freezer and place half of it in the air fryer basket.

5. Set the trivet in the dry pressure cooker pot and place the fryer basket on top. Now set the CrispLid on the inner pot and plug it in. Set to 360°F and air fry 20 minutes, tossing halfway.

6. Cook until crispy and lightly browned. Toss with the sauce and serve, garnished with green onion

Per Serving: Calories 81; Carbs: 16g; Total Fat 1g; Protein 2g; Cholesterol: 0mg; Fiber: 1g

Chicken Bacon Ranch Poppers

Chicken meatballs stuffed with cheese and wrapped in bacon. Great lunch idea!

Prep Time: 10 minutes

Cook Time: 15 minutes

Servings: 20 yields

Ingredients

1 pound ground chicken

6 strips of uncooked bacon

1/2 cup of bread crumbs

1 egg

1/2 cup of Provolone cheese

12 1" squares of cheddar cheese

3 tablespoons of ranch dip seasoning

Directions

1. In a bowl, add together the ground chicken, bread crumbs, egg, cheese, and the Ranch seasoning until well combined.

2. Now shape into balls of about an inch. Place a cheddar square firmly in the center. Wrap a bacon around each of the meatball.

3. Place in the fryer basket and arrange in a single layer, (work in batches). Set the Crisplid on the pot and plug it in. Set temperature to cook for 15 minutes at 350°F.

4. Cool and serve!

Per Serving: Calories 96; Total Fat 6g; Protein 8g; Total Carb 2g; Cholesterol: 41mg

Crispy Kale Chips

A nutritious low-calorie snack, made even healthier by crisp frying.

Prep Time: 5 minutes

Cook Time: 15minutes

Servings: 4

Ingredients:

1 kale head

Cooking spray

1 teaspoon soya sauce

Directions:

1. Remove the center steam of the kale and tear up into pieces of 1½ inches. Wash these pieces and dry.

2. Place in the fryer basket. Toss with the soya sauce and generously with cooking spray. Set the trivet in the pressure cooker. Place the fryer basket on the trivet.

3. Set the Crisp Lid on the pot and plug it in. Set temperature to 400°F and set to cook for 15 minutes. Toss after 10 minutes and keep cooking until edges are brown, not burnt. Enjoy!

Per Serving: Calories 58; Total Fat 2.8g; Protein 2.5g; Total Carb 7.6g; Cholesterol: 0mg

Crispy Mozzarella Sticks

Enjoy healthy!

Prep Time: 20 minutes

Cook Time: 15minutes

Servings: 4

Ingredients:

For the Batter:

1/2 cup of water

1/4 cup flour

1 tablespoon cornmeal

5 tablespoons of cornstarch

1 teaspoon garlic powder

1/2 teaspoon salt

Coating:

1 cup panko bread crumbs

1/2 teaspoon ground black pepper

1/2 teaspoon salt

1/2 teaspoon parsley flakes

1/4 teaspoon onion powder

1/2 teaspoon garlic powder

1/4 teaspoon dried basil

1/4 teaspoon dried oregano

5 oz. mozzarella cheese, strips

1 tablespoon of all-purpose flour

Cooking spray

Directions

1. Combine the flour, cornmeal, cornstarch, garlic powder, salt and water in a bowl and then mix until the batter attains a pancake-like consistency.

2. In a separate bowl, add together the panko, parsley, onion powder, basil, oregano, garlic powder, salt and pepper.

3. Coat each mozzarella sticks lightly with flour, dip in batter and toss to coat in the panko mixture. Place all the sticks on a baking sheet, in a single layer and freeze for 1-2 hours.

4. Arrange mozzarella sticks in the fryer basket. Spray with cooking spray. Set the trivet in the pressure cooker. Place the fryer basket on the trivet. Set the Crisp Lid on the pot and plug it in. Set temperature to 450°F and set to cook for 5 minutes. Flip with tongs and cook for 7- 10 minutes.

5. Season with garlic salt. Enjoy, serve with marinara sauce.

Per Serving: Calories 246; Total Fat 6.8g; Protein 12.9g; Total Carb 39.2g; Cholesterol: 23mg

Easy Ground Beef Empanadas
Juicy baked beef empanadas – great for a party!

Prep Time: 15 minutes

Cook Time: 15 minutes

Servings: 24

Ingredients

2 tablespoons of oil

1 small onion diced

2 garlic cloves, minced

1 lb. ground beef

3/4 cup green onion, chopped

1/4 cup cilantro, chopped

1/4 cup parsley, chopped

2 tablespoon smoked paprika

1/2 tablespoon ground cumin

3/4 teaspoon of freshly ground black pepper

Salt

1 cup tomato sauce

1 box of pie crusts refrigerated

Directions

1. Let pie crust sit at room temperature for 15 minutes.

2. Place pressure cooker on sauté and then once add the oil. Sauté onion and garlic and then add the beef and sauté until browned.

3. Add spices, parsley, green onion, cilantro and the tomato sauce. Stir thoroughly to combine and let it cook 5 minutes or less. Turn off pressure cooker. Drain the fat and transfer to a bowl; Cool 5 minutes.

4. Now, roll out a pie crust and cut into rounds with a biscuit cutter. Put a tablespoon of the meat mixture in the center of each crust round and then brush with water, fold over the filling and seal edges by crimping with a fork. Repeat process with the other pie crust.

5. Whisk an egg, 1 tbsp water and a dash of ground black pepper together. Brush tops of the empanadas lightly with the egg wash and spray with cook spray.

6. Place the empanadas in the fryer basket and arrange in a single layer, (work in batches). Set the Crisplid on the pot and plug it in. Set temperature to cook for 4 minutes at 400°F. Flip with tongs and cook another 4 minutes. Repeat with the reserved empanadas. Cool and serve!

Nutrition info: Calories 74; Total Fat 5.6g; Protein 3.7g; Net Carb 2.3g; Fiber: 0.6g

Cheesy Hasselback Potatoes

Enjoy potatoes the hasselback way! Buttery and crispy, these sliced side- dishes are easy to make and will make you ask for more! Simply place the potato between 2 wooden spoons and slice away. Once you do, you'll find it easy to cut the potato all through. Bake and insert the cheese slices.

Prep Time: 10minutes

Cook Time: 1 hour

Servings: 4

Ingredients

4 medium-sized Russet potatoes

2 tbsp of melted unsalted butter

Salt & pepper to taste

12 slices of cheddar cheese, cut thinly into 1-inch

1/3 cup Parmesan cheese, shredded

1 tablespoon chopped fresh chives

Directions

1. Slice each potato about 1/8 to 1/4 inch apart; do not cut all the way through. Brush with melted butter and season also with salt and pepper.

2. Place the potatoes in the fryer basket and then set the trivet in the pressure cooker. Place the fryer basket on the trivet.

3. Set the Crisp Lid on the pot and plug it in. Set temperature to 400°F and set to cook for 40 minutes. Flip with tongs after 10 minutes and keep cooking.

4. After 10 minutes remove, and place the cheddar slices in the potato cuts. Sprinkle with Parmesan and keep baking and flipping until cheese is melted and potatoes are crispy.

5. Cool and serve, garnished with chives or parsley.

Nutrition info: Calories 247; Total Fat 7g; Protein 6.1g; Total Carb 41.1g; Cholesterol: 19mg

Nacho Covered Prawns

Prep time: 30 minutes

Cooking time: 8 minutes

Servings: 3

Ingredients:

9 ounces nacho chips

1 egg, beaten

18 medium sized prawns

Directions:

1. Remove the prawn's shell and veins, wash thoroughly and wipe dry.

2. Grind the chips like breadcrumbs and then dip each prawn into the egg and coat with the chip crumbs.

3. Add prawns, (if necessary, in batches) to the fryer basket. Place trivet in pressure cooker pot and place the basket in pot. Set the Crisp lid on the pot and plug it.

4. Spray basket with cook spray and cook for 8 minutes at 356°F. Serve with salsa or sour cream.

Per Serving: Calories 581; Total Fat 25g; Protein 33g; Total Carb 58g; Cholesterol: 62mg; Fiber:9g

Stuffed Mushrooms With Sour Cream

A great dish! The sour cream and cheese hold the stuffing together!

Prep Time: 30 minutes

Cook Time: 15 minutes

Servings: 24

Ingredients

24 mushrooms, caps & stems diced

1/2 onion, diced

1/2 orange bell pepper, diced

1 small carrot, diced

2 bacon slices, diced

1 cup cheddar cheese, shredded

1/2 cup of sour cream

1 1/2 tablespoons of Cheddar cheese, shredded

Directions

1. Press the sauté function of your pressure cooker. Add the mushroom stems, carrot, orange bell pepper, onion, and bacon to the inner pot and cook for about 5 minutes until softened.

2. Add the cup of shredded cheddar cheese and sour cream. Stir and cook for a couple of minutes until cheese is melted and stuffing is thoroughly combined. Turn off pressure cooker.

3. Arrange the mushroom caps on the pressure cooker basket, in batches. Heap the stuffing to the mushroom cap and sprinkle with Cheddar cheese.

4. Place trivet in the inner steel pot of your pressure cooker. Place the basket on the trivet. Set the Crisp Lid on the pot and plug it in. Set temperature to 350°F and set to cook for 8 minutes.

Nutrition info: Calories 43; Total Fat 3.1g; Protein 2.4g; Total Carb 1.7g; Cholesterol: 8mg

Kerala Fried Chicken

An addictive appetizer dish made flavorful by marinating the chicken in buttermilk brine and a puree and a puree of ginger, garlic cloves, curry, serrano peppers and cilantro and coated in batter. Enjoy in a sandwich or dipped in sauce of choice.

Prep Time: 20minutes

Cook Time: 8 minutes

Servings: 8

Ingredients

Chicken and Marinade

2 lbs boneless, skinless chicken thighs

1/2 cup of fresh cilantro leaves

1 cup of buttermilk

3 serrano chile peppers, stemmed

1 inch fresh ginger piece, peeled

16 curry leaves

4 cloves garlic

1 1/2 teaspoons salt, or to taste

Coating

1 cup rolled oats

6 tablespoons rice flour

4 teaspoons of whole black peppercorns

6 tablespoons of all-purpose flour

3 teaspoons salt, divided

4 teaspoons coconut oil

Directions

1. Prep the chicken by cutting in half, trimming excess fat and the pounding the pieces to make them flat. Once done, place in a bowl.

2. Add together the buttermilk, serrano chile peppers, cilantro, the ginger, curry leaves, garlic, and 1½ teaspoons salt in food processor and puree until well mixed and the pour over chicken. Cover and place in the refrigerator to marinate for 5- 12 hours.

3. Process the rolled oats and peppercorns in a food processor until blended. Add the flour, rice flour and the remaining salt. Remove to a bowl.

4. Take out the chicken from the marinade and dip in the oat mixture to coat evenly, shaking off excess oat mixture.

5. Now set the trivet in the pressure cooker's inner steel pot and place the fryer basket on it (the trivet). Place the coated chicken pieces in the basket, (in batches, do not overcrowd basket). Drizzle over with coconut oil

6. Set the Crisp lid on the pot and plug it in. Cook at 450°F for 8-10 minutes. Use a meat thermometer to ensure it reads 165°F or more, before removing. Airfry the rest of the chicken as well. Enjoy!

Per Serving: Calories 302; Total Fat 12g; Protein 31g; Total Carb 15.5g; Cholesterol: 139mg

Crispy Fried Onion Rings

Simple and crispy onion rings that you can enjoy topped to your burger for that crunchy taste and also add to your favorite salads to give it that crunch.

Prep Time: 20minutes

Cook Time: 10minutes

Serves: 12

Ingredients

1/2 cup all-purpose flour

1/2 cup of water

1 egg, beaten lightly

1 teaspoon of seasoned salt

Pinch cayenne pepper

1/2 teaspoon baking powder

1 large onion, thinly sliced

Cooking spray

Directions

1. Combine the flour, water, egg, salt and baking powder in a bowl.

2. Separate the onion slices into rings and then dip into batter.

3. Spray fryer basket and onion rings with cooking spray and place the rings in the basket, in a single layer. (Do this in batches).

4. Place trivet in pressure cooker's inner steel pot and place the fryer basket on the trivet. Set the Crisp lid on the pot and plug it.

5. Set to cook at 400°F for 5 minutes and then flip. Keep again for 5 minutes until crispy and browned. Cook the rest of the onion rings. Serve immediately.

Per Serving: Calories 71; Total Fat 5g; Protein 1g; Total Carb 5g; Cholesterol: 18mg

Buffalo-Ranch Chickpeas

An easy- to- make highly addictive spicy snack!

Prep Time: 5minutes

Cook Time: 20minutes

Serves: 2

Ingredients

1 (15 oz) can chickpeas, drained &rinsed

2 tablespoons of Buffalo wing sauce

1 tablespoon of dry ranch dressing mix

Directions

1. Spread chickpeas over a lined baking sheet. Remove excess moisture by pressing the chickpeas with paper towels.

2. Place the chickpeas in a bowl. Add the Buffalo wing sauce and then toss. Add the ranch dressing powder and thoroughly mix.

3. Transfer chickpeas to basket evenly. Place trivet in pressure cooker's inner steel pot and place the fryer basket on the trivet. Set the Crisp lid on the pot and plug it.

5. Set to cook at 350°F for 8 minutes and then shake. Cook for an additional 5 minutes. Shake again and cook 5 more minutes. Finally, shake and cook for 2 minutes. Cool and serve immediately.

Per Serving: Calories 177; Total Fat 1.6g; Protein 7g; Total Carb 33.6g; Cholesterol: 0mg

Buffalo Cauliflower Bites

A delicious side dish. Always a hit!

Prep Time: 40 minutes

Cook Time: 42 minutes

Servings: 6

Ingredients

2 heads cauliflower, trimmed & cut in florets (about 2")

1 1/2 cups water

1 1/2 cups cornstarch

2 teaspoons baking powder

1/2 cup all-purpose flour

1 teaspoon garlic powder

1 teaspoon kosher salt

1 teaspoon onion powder

1 teaspoon black pepper

2 eggs

1/3 cup buffalo wing sauce

Directions

1. Combine ½ cup of water and cauliflower in the inner pot of your pressure cooker. Place the lid on and seal the pressure release valve.

2. Cook on low pressure for minutes. Perform a quick release afterwards, remove lid, drain cauliflower and place in the refrigerator to chill for 10 minutes. Unplug pressure cooker.

3. Combine in a medium bowl, the cornstarch, baking powder, flour, onion powder, garlic powder, salt and pepper. Whisk in the egg and a cup of water until smooth. Add the chilled cauliflower as well, and toss to coat. Place on a baking sheet and return to chill in the freezer for 25 minutes.

4. Now place the cauliflower in the fryer basket of your pressure cooker, (in batches). Place trivet in pressure cooker's inner steel pot and place the fryer basket on the trivet. Set the Crisp lid on the pot and plug it.

5. Set to cook at 360°F for 25 minutes and then toss halfway. Remove cauliflower once crisp and golden. Repeat process for the remaining chilled cauliflower.

6. When ready to serve, warm hot sauce in the microwave for 40 seconds, toss with cooked cauliflower and enjoy!

Per Serving: Calories 249; Total Fat 4g; Protein 7g; Total Carb 58g; Cholesterol: 62mg; Fiber:5g

Simple Cajun Shrimp

Prep Time: 2minutes

Cook Time: 6minutes

Servings: 2

Ingredients

1/2 pound shrimp, peeled & deveined

1/4 teaspoon of cayenne pepper

1/4 teaspoon smoked paprika

Pinch salt

1/2 teaspoon old bay seasoning

Directions

1. Combine all ingredients in a bowl and mix thoroughly to coat shrimp.

2. Transfer to fryer basket. Set Trivet in pressure cooker pot and place basket on trivet. Set the Crisp lid on the pot and plug it.

3. Set at 390°F for 6 minutes, checking and flipping half way through.

Per Serving: Calories 68; Total Fat 0g; Protein 28g; Total Carb 0g; Cholesterol: 173mg; Fiber:0g

Chicken Fritter

Ground chicken meat mix with some spices, dill, cheese and bread crumbs, formed into a patties, and cooked with your CrispLid makes this dish a great one.

Prep Time: 5 minutes

Cook Time: 10 minutes

Servings: 6

Ingredients

1 pound ground chicken or chicken breast, chopped finely

1/4 cup parmesan cheese, shredded

1/4 cup provolone cheese, shredded

1 teaspoon onion powder

1 teaspoon garlic powder

1 teaspoon salt

1 teaspoon pepper

1/2 cup panko bread crumbs

3 chopped green onions

1 tablespoon of dill

Directions

1. Combine the ground chicken, the cheese, green onions and the seasonings in a bowl and make into patties.

2. Place in fryer basket. Set the trivet in the pot of the pressure cooker. Place the fryer basket on the trivet and then set the Crisp lid on the pot and plug it in.

3. Set temperature to 375°F for 10 minutes cook time. Serve with dipping sauce of choice.

Per Serving: Calories 202; Total Fat 6g; Protein 27g; Total Carb 9g; Cholesterol: 71mg; Fiber:1g

Texas Cheese Fries In Melted Cheese
Prep Time: 5 minutes

Cook Time: 25 minutes

Servings: 2

Ingredients

1 package (2 lb. bag) of seasoned frozen French fries

4 slices of bacon

1 cup mozzarella cheese, shredded

1 cup cheddar cheese, shredded

For dipping: Ranch dressing

Directions

1. Place your pressure cooker unit on sauté to preheat and after 5 minutes, sauté the bacon until crispy. Remove and turn off function. Unplug pressure cooker.

2. Place French fries in pressure cooker basket and place in the pot. Set Trivet in pressure cooker pot and place basket on trivet. Set the Crisp lid on the pot and plug it.

3. Set at 375°F for 20minutes. Sprinkle cheeses at the last 2 minutes and continue cooking. Remove, top with crumbled bacon and enjoy dipped with ranch dressing.

Per Serving: Calories 1368; Total Fat 84g; Protein 43g; Total Carb 121g; Cholesterol: 151mg; Fiber:5g

Spicy Dill Pickle Fries
A sure pleaser!

Prep Time: 15 minutes

Cook Time: 15 minutes

Servings: 12

Ingredients

1 1/2 (16 oz.) jars spicy dill pickle spears

1 cup flour

1/2 teaspoon of paprika

1 egg, beaten

1/4 cup milk

1 cup panko bread crumbs

Cooking spray

Directions

1. Drain the pickles and pat dry with paper towels.

2. In a bowl, add together the flour and paprika. In a separate bowl, whisk the egg and add the milk, mixing well. Place the panko in a third bowl.

3. Dip the pickle in the flour mix, and then the egg mix, and finally the bread crumbs to coat fully and then place on a plate. Once all the pickles are coated, spray with cooking spray and transfer to the pressure cooker fryer basket.

4. Set the trivet in the pot of the pressure cooker. Place the fryer basket on the trivet and then set the Crisp lid on the pot and plug it in. Set temperature to 350°F and cook for 14 minutes, flipping halfway.

5. Serve with your favorite dipping sauce.

Per Serving: Calories 80; Total Fat 1g; Protein 3g; Total Carb 16.8g; Cholesterol: 16mg;

Quick & Easy Crispy Tofu

Crispy, firm and delicious! The perfect appetizer in just 30 minutes! Can also be a perfect side dish to a salad or a stir-fry. Enjoy!

Prep Time: 10 minutes

Cook Time: 20 minutes

Servings: 2

Ingredients

16 ounces extra firm tofu

1 pinch sea salt

1 teaspoon curry powder or chili powder

1 tablespoon coconut oil

Directions

1. Wrap the tofu in an absorbent towel, press to remove excess water by setting something heavy on it. Unwrap, pat dry and remove to a bowl.

2. Drizzle oil over the tofu as well as the salt and seasoning.

3. Arrange in CrispLid fryer basket, in batches, and ensure it is placed in a single layer. Set the trivet in the pot of the pressure cooker. Place the fryer basket on the trivet and then set the Crisp lid on the pot and plug it in.

3. Set temperature to 350°F and cook for 10 minutes; flip tofu using tongs and continue cooking until crispy.

Per Serving: Calories 225; Total Fat 17g; Protein 18.6g; Total Carb 3.8g; Fiber:2g

Honey Garlic Chicken Wings

Crispy chicken wings that's good enough for a party!

Prep Time: 5 minutes

Cook Time: 20 minutes

Servings: 10

Ingredients

11/2 lbs. chicken wings

2 tablespoons soy sauce

1/ 4 cup of potato starch

3 garlic cloves

1 tablespoon butter

3 tablespoon honey

1/2 teaspoon of salt

¾ teaspoon of red pepper flakes

Directions

1. Toss chicken with soy sauce. Set to one side.

2. In a large Ziploc bag, add the potato starch and the wings and shake to coat wings evenly with the starch.

3. Grease the fryer basket with some oil. Arrange wings, in batches, and ensure it is placed in a single layer. Set the trivet in the pot of the pressure cooker. Place the fryer basket on the trivet and then set the Crisp lid on the pot and plug it in.

4. Set temperature to cook at 400°F for 20 minutes. After 15 minutes, flip cook for 5 more minutes.

5. To make your sauce, melt butter and garlic in a microwave. Add the honey, stir and add salt and red pepper flakes. Toss in the chicken wings and serve.

Per Serving: Calories 262; Total Fat 7g; Protein 11g; Total Carb 14g; Fiber:1g; Cholesterol: 26mg

Asian Barbecue Satay

Prep Time: 15minutes

Cook Time: 15 minutes

Servings: 3

Ingredients

4 garlic cloves, chopped

¾ pound (12 oz.) chicken tenders, boneless & skinless

½ cup pineapple juice

½ cup soy sauce

¼ cup of sesame oil

4 scallions, chopped

2 teaspoons sesame seeds, toasted

1 tablespoon fresh ginger, grated

Pinch black pepper

Directions

1. Skewer the chicken tender, trimming excess fat.

2. Combine remaining ingredients in a bowl. Add the skewered chicken to it. Combine well, cover and chill 2 to 24hours.

3. Pat dry chicken. Arrange the skewers to the fryer basket, in batches in a single layer. Set the trivet in the pot of the pressure cooker. Place the fryer basket on the trivet and then set the Crisp lid on the pot and plug it in.

3. Set temperature to 400°F and cook for 15minutes

Per Serving: Calories 357; Total Fat 20g; Protein 32g; Total Carb 14g; Fiber:2g; Cholesterol: 55mg;

Asparagus Fries

A tasty vegetarian appetizer that consist of coated asparagus spears cooked in a crispy way and dipped in dipping sauce of choice.

Prep Time: 20 minutes

Cook Time: 10 minutes

Servings: 4

Ingredients

1 cup bread crumbs

1/4 teaspoons freshly ground black pepper

1/4 teaspoons kosher salt

1/2 cup all-purpose flour

1 lb. asparagus spears, trimmed

2 large eggs, beaten lightly

Cooking spray

Directions

1. In a shallow bowl, add together the bread crumbs, salt, and black pepper. In a separate shallow bowl, place the flour.

2. Coat the asparagus spears in flour, shake any excess off and dip in eggs. Let any excess drip off. Place the asparagus in the bread crumb mixture and then press gently to coat. Coat in cooking spray generously.

3. Place in fryer basket, in batches. Set the trivet in the pot of the pressure cooker. Place the fryer basket on the trivet and then set the Crisp lid on the pot and plug it in.

4. Cook at 400°F for 10 minutes. After 5 minutes, flip asparagus and cook until golden brown. Serve, with your favorite dipping sauce.

Per Serving: Calories 225; Total Fat 4g; Protein 11g; Total Carb 36.3g; Cholesterol: 93mg; Fiber:1g

Air Fried Bacon Wrapped Asparagus

An irresistible meal of tender asparagus wrapped in excellently-cooked bacon. Using your CrispLid makes it even nicer and crispy. Enjoy this salty and savory meal!

Prep Time: 5 minutes

Cook Time: 10 minutes

Servings: 10 yields

Ingredients

1 bunch fresh asparagus

Olive oil spray

10 slices bacon, uncooked, cut in half

Directions

1. Wrap a bacon piece around 2 asparagus stalks and spray all the pieces with olive oil and a sprinkle of salt.

2. Place in fryer basket, in batches. Set the trivet in the pot of the pressure cooker. Place the fryer basket on the trivet and then set the Crisp lid on the pot and plug it in.

3. Set at a temperature of 390°F for 10 minutes.

Per Serving: Calories 127; Total Fat 12g; Protein 4g; Total Carb 0g; Cholesterol: 18mg; Fiber:0g

Apple Chips In Coconut Cream

A healthy apple snack in 20 minutes!

Prep Time: 18 minutes

Cook Time: 10 minutes

Servings: 8

Ingredients

2 teaspoons ground cinnamon

1/4 cup white sugar

4 apples, cut with a mandolin in thick pieces of ⅛inches

2 cup chilled coconut cream

1/4 cup maple syrup

8 teaspoons lemon juice

4 teaspoons vanilla extract

Directions

1. Combine cinnamon and sugar in a bowl. Dip the apple slices in the mixture to coat on one side only.

2. Place coated apple slices in fryer basket, in batches. Set the trivet in the pot of the pressure cooker. Place the fryer basket on the trivet and then set the Crisp lid on the pot and plug it in.

3. Set temperature to 375°F for 4 minutes cook time. Flip and cook another 4 minutes until lightly browned.

4. In a bowl, whisk the coconut cream with an electric mixer until fluffy. Add the maple syrup, lemon juice, as well as the vanilla extract and then stir to mix well.

5. Remove to a bowl; cool and serve with coconut cream dip.

Per Serving: Calories 370; Total Fat 12g; Protein 1g; Total Carb 65.8g; Cholesterol: 0mg; Fiber:0g

Chicken Sandwich

These juicy tender chicken sandwiches are the real deal!

Prep Time: 5 minutes

Cook Time: 25 minutes

Servings: 4

Ingredients

1 lb. chicken breast, quartered

1 cup pickle juice

1 cup of flour

1 teaspoon of paprika

1 teaspoon of garlic powder

1 teaspoon basil

1 teaspoon pepper

1 teaspoon salt

Cooking Spray

1/2 cup of milk

1 egg

Directions

1. Combine the chicken pieces and pickle juice in a bowl and leave to marinate for an hour.

2. Add together the dry ingredients in a bowl. Whisk together the egg and milk and then dredge chicken in flour mixture and then the egg. Dip again in flour to coat well.

3. Place in the fryer basket and spray with cooking spray. Place the trivet in the pressure cooker inner steel pot and place the basket on the trivet.

4. Set the Crisp lid on the pot and plug it in. Cook at 360°F for 20 minutes, until the internal temperature of the chicken reads 160°F

Per Serving: Calories 420; Total Fat 10g; Protein 41g; Total Carb 39g; Cholesterol: 145mg; Fiber:1g

Sweet Potato Fries

A quick and easy recipe. Its use of little oil makes it healthy too! Enjoy as an appetizer or snack.

Prep Time: 10 minutes

Cook Time: 16 minutes

Servings: 8

Ingredients

8 large sweet potatoes, cut thickly into strips

2 teaspoons garlic powder

2 teaspoons of salt

2 teaspoons of chili powder

1 teaspoons of ground cumin

1/2 cup canola oil

Directions

1. In a large bowl, add together the garlic powder, cumin, salt and chili powder. Add the olive oil, whisk and then add the potato strips. Toss all to coat.

2. Place in the fryer basket in a single layer, (in batches, if necessary), to ensure and even cooking. Set the trivet in the pot of the pressure cooker. Place the fryer basket on the trivet and then set the Crisp lid on the pot and plug it in.

3. Set temperature to 425°F for 20 minutes cook time. Repeat process for the remaining potato strips. Enjoy!

Per Serving: Calories 240; Total Fat 14g; Protein 2g; Total Carb 27.8g; Cholesterol: 0mg; Fiber:0g

Upside-Down Stuffed Chicken Nachos

Put your pressure cooker and Crisp lid to work by making these rich crunchy cheesy chicken nachos.

Prep Time: 10 minutes

Cook Time: 25 minutes

Servings: 8

Ingredients

4 frozen boneless skinless chicken breasts (12 oz. each or less)

1 jar (16 oz.) red salsa

1 can (14 oz.) refried beans

1 tablespoon salt

2 tablespoons taco seasoning

1 1/2 bags (12 oz.) Mexican cheese blend, divided

1/4 bag (4 oz.) tortilla chips, divided

For toppings:

Sour cream

Guacamole

Fresh scallions, sliced

Directions

1. Place the frozen chicken and the salsa in the inner pot of your pressure cooker. Seal the lid and ensure the valve is set to the sealing position. Cook 20 minutes on high and then perform a quick release.

2. Open lid and shred chicken. Add the refried beans, taco seasoning and salt, and stir to incorporate well. Turn off pressure cooker.

3. Place half of the tortilla chips in an even layer on the chicken mixture and then add half of the cheese to cover the cheese. Do the same with the rest of the tortilla chips, placing it as a second layer and topping with the remaining cheese.

4. Set the Crisp lid on the pot and plug it in. Cook at 360°F for 5-10 minutes. Serve nachos, garnished with guacamole, sour cream &scallions.

Per Serving: Calories 512; Total Fat 23g; Protein 50g; Total Carb 26g; Cholesterol:150mg; Fiber:7g

Air Crisp Mashed Potato Pancakes

Use up leftover potatoes in the most delicious way. Make flavorful mashed potato pancakes that are crispy on the outside, yet fluffy and creamy at the center. You'd definitely ask for more!

Prep Time: 5 minutes

Cook Time: 15 minutes

Servings: 1

Ingredients

2 cups of mashed potatoes

2 strips of cooked bacon

1 cup of cheddar cheese

1 egg

1 green onions, chopped

2 tablespoons of all- purpose flour

1 cup of panko bread crumbs

Salt and Pepper

Directions

1. Combine in a bowl; potatoes, bacon, cheese, egg, green onions, a little salt and pepper, as well as the flour. Form into a patty and coat in bread crumbs.

2. Transfer to freezer to solidify for 15 minutes.

3. Cover pressure cooker basket with foil, add firm patty. Set the trivet in pot. Set the Crisp lid on the pot and plug it in. Cook at 390°F for 7 minutes.

4. Flip over and cook for an additional 5 minutes.

Per Serving: Calories 273; Total Fat 13g; Protein 11g; Total Carb 28g; Cholesterol:56mg; Fiber:2g

Air Fried Rosemary Chips

A crunchier version of your regular chips!

Prep time: 40 minutes

Cook time: 30minutes

Servings: 4

Ingredients:

2 teaspoons of nicely chopped rosemary

4 russet potatoes

Cooking spray

¼ teaspoon of salt

Directions:

1. Peel potatoes, slice into chips and soak 30 minutes in water. Drain and pat dry.

2. Spray fryer basket with cooking spray, add potato chip in single layer and spray.

3. Place trivet in pressure cooker's inner steel pot and place the fryer basket on the trivet. Set the Crisp lid on the pot and plug it.

4. Set to cook at 375°F for 30 minutes. Flip half way through cooking and cook until golden and crisp. Remove, add the rosemary and salt and toss to mix.

Per Serving: Calories 115; Total Fat 3.5g; Protein 2.2g; Total Carb 19.2g; Cholesterol: 0mg

Green Bean Fries With Garlic and Parmesan

Easy to make, these snacks made with readily available ingredients, are just right for many occasions.

Prep time: 5 minutes

Cook time: 5minutes

Servings: 12

Ingredients:

1 pound fresh green beans

1 cup panko bread crumbs

1/2 cup parm cheese

1 tbs garlic powder

2 eggs

1/2 cup flour

Directions

1. Begin by rinsing the beans and then coating it in flour.

2. Whisk the eggs and dip the green beans in it.

3. Combine the panko bread crumbs, garlic powder and cheese in a bowl and then dip the beans in the mixture as well to coat thoroughly. Transfer to basket.

4. Place trivet in pressure cooker's inner steel pot and place the fryer basket on the trivet. Set the Crisp lid on the pot and plug it.

5. Set to cook at 390°F for 5 minutes. Sprinkle with extra cheese.

Per Serving: Calories 98; Total Fat 3g; Protein 5g; Total Carb 14g; Cholesterol: 35mg; Fiber: 2g

Crispy Taco Pie

Cheesy layers of taco goodness!

Prep time: 10 minutes

Cook time: 5minutes

Servings: 6

Ingredients:

6 Tortilla Shells

1 can of refried beans

1 lb. ground beef

2 cups of cheddar cheese

Taco Seasonings

Directions

1. Press the sauté function of your pressure cooker. Add cooking spray and cook the ground beef until browned turn off sauté. Add in water and the taco seasonings. Add a tortilla shell as well.

2. Spread a layer of refried beans thinly and top with a layer of taco meat, and then the cheese. Continue with the process until full and finally top with a tortilla cheese and plenty of cheese. Unplug pressure cooker

3. Set the Crisp lid on the pot and plug it. Set to cook at 450°F for 5 minutes. Top with desired toppings such as sour cream, green onions tomatoes, lettuce and salsa.

Per Serving: Calories 628; Total Fat 39g; Protein 41g; Total Carb 28g; Cholesterol: 131mg; Fiber: 6g

Crispy Moroccan Chickpeas

Prep Time: 5 minutes

Cook Time: 20 minutes

Servings: 4

Ingredients

2 cans (15 ounces each) chickpeas, rinsed, drained

2 tablespoons extra virgin olive oil, divided

1 teaspoon kosher salt, plus more for seasoning

2 teaspoons garam masala

1/2 teaspoon garlic powder

1 teaspoon of paprika

1/4 teaspoon of ground mustard powder

Directions

1. Dry the chickpeas thoroughly and place in a bowl. Add a tablespoon of oil and salt and then toss to coat.

2. Press the sauté function of your pressure cooker. Add the chickpeas and sauté for about 5 minutes until golden brown. Unplug pressure cooker.

3. Combine the chickpeas, the remaining oil and the seasonings and toss. Place in the fryer basket. Place trivet in pot. Place basket on it. Set the CrispLid on the inner steel pot of the pressure cooker ad plug in.

4. Set temperature for 400°F and cook time for 15 minutes. Toss half way through cooking.

5. Remove and serve immediately.

Per Serving: Calories 89; Total Fat 8g; Protein 3g; Total Carb 5g; Cholesterol: 0mg; Fiber: 1g

The End

Made in the
USA
Monee, IL

15899995R00066